MARK | *Jesus*

Marilyn Kunz
& Catherine Schell

18 Discussions for Group Bible Study

Neighborhood Bible Studies Publishers
Dobbs Ferry, NY

neighborhood bible studies

Discover

Jesus

MARK

Marilyn Kunz

& Catherine Schell

18 Discussions for Group Bible Study

Neighborhood Bible Studies Publishers
Dobbs Ferry, NY 10522

neighborhood bible studies

ISBN 1-880266-14-8
Second Printing 2002
Printed in the United States of America
Illustrations by Alex Bishop
Cover photo by Russell and Lynn Hudson

CONTENTS

HOW TO USE THIS DISCUSSION GUIDE

T his study guide uses the inductive approach to Bible study. *It will help you discover for yourself what the Bible says.* It will not give you prepackaged answers. *People remember most what they discover for themselves and what they express in their own words.* The study guide provides three kinds of questions:

1. What does the passage say? What are the facts?
2. What is the meaning of these facts?
3. How does this passage apply to your life?

- Observe the facts carefully before you interpret the meaning of your observations. Then apply the truths you have discovered to life today. Resist the temptation to skip the fact questions since we are not as observant as we think. Find the facts quickly so you can spend more time on their meaning and application.

- *The purpose of Bible study is not just to know more Bible truths but to apply them.* Allow these truths to make a difference in how you think and act, in your attitudes and relationships, in the quality and direction of your life.

- Each discussion requires about one hour. Decide on the amount of time to add for socializing and prayer.

- *Share the leadership.* If a different person is the moderator or question-asker each week, interest grows and members feel the group belongs to everyone. The Bible is the authority in the group, not the question-asker.

- When a group grows to more than ten, the quiet people become quieter. Plan to grow and multiply. You can meet as two groups in the same house or begin another group so that more people can participate and benefit.

TOOLS FOR AN EFFECTIVE BIBLE STUDY

1. A study guide for each person in the group.

2. A modern translation of the Bible such as:
    NEW INTERNATIONAL VERSION (NIV)
    CONTEMPORARY ENGLISH VERSION (CEV)
    JERUSALEM BIBLE (JB)
    NEW AMERICAN STANDARD BIBLE (NASB)
    REVISED ENGLISH BIBLE (REB)
    NEW REVISED STANDARD VERSION (NRSV)

3. An English dictionary.

4. A map of the Lands of the Bible in a Bible or in the study guide.

5. Your conviction that the Bible is worth studying.

GUIDELINES FOR AN EFFECTIVE STUDY

1. Stick to the passage under discussion.

2. Avoid tangents. If the subject is not addressed in the passage, put it on hold until after the study.

3. Let the Bible speak for itself. Do not quote other authorities or rewrite it to say what you want it to say.

4. Apply the passage personally and honestly.

5. Listen to one another to sharpen your insights.

6. Prepare by reading the Bible passage and thinking through the questions during the week.

7. Begin and end on time.

HELPS FOR THE QUESTION-ASKER

1. Prepare by reading the passage several times, using different translations if possible. Ask for God's help in understanding it. Consider how the questions might be answered. Observe which questions can be answered quickly and which may require more time.

2. Begin on time.

3. Lead the group in opening prayer or ask someone ahead of time to do so. Don't take anyone by surprise.

4. Ask for a different volunteer to read each Bible section. Read the question. Wait for an answer. Rephrase the question if necessary. Resist the temptation to answer the question yourself. Move to the next question. Skip questions already answered by the discussion.

5. Encourage everyone to participate. Ask the group, "What do the rest of you think?" "What else could be added?"

6. Receive all answers warmly. If needed, ask, "In which verse did you find that?" "How does that fit with verse...?"

7. If a tangent arises, ask, "Do we find the answer to that here?" Or suggest, "Let's write that down and look for the information as we go along."

8. Discourage members who are too talkative by saying, "When I read the next question, let's hear from someone who hasn't spoken yet today."

9. Use the summary questions to bring the study to a conclusion on time.

10. Close the study with prayer.

11. Decide on one person to be the host and another person to ask the questions at the next discussion.

INTRODUCTION *to the Gospel of* MARK

Would you like to have heard the Apostle Peter tell about his experiences with Jesus? Read the Gospel according to Mark! Written about 65 A.D., Mark's Gospel is the earliest record we have of the life of Jesus. It contains Peter's eyewitness account which Mark recorded from Peter's preaching and teaching.

We know about the author, John Mark, from brief mentions in the book of Acts, the letters of Paul and Peter, and from what is probably his personal signature in Mark 14:51, 52. Mark accompanied his relative Barnabas and the Apostle Paul on the first missionary journey but deserted the trip before it ended. Paul refused to take Mark on his second journey, but spoke highly of him later (2 Timothy 4:11) indicating Mark's stature as a Christian leader in later years. Peter called him *my son Mark* (1 Peter 5:13). The Christians in Jerusalem used the house of Mark's mother Mary as their headquarters.

The Gospel of Mark is the shortest of the four records of the life of Jesus. Its vivid realism presents Jesus as fully divine and fully human. Mark devoted six out of sixteen chapters to the last week in Jesus' life, indicating the importance of these particular events. Mark wrote for the Gentile Roman mind presenting Jesus as the Christ, the Son of God. A careful examination of the record requires a definite response to the facts presented. William Barclay comments that Mark's Gospel could be called the most important book in the world.

Jesus' Early Ministry

MARK 1

During the events of Mark's Gospel, Roman legions are keeping the peace in an empire that extends from Britain in the west to Persia in the east. John the Baptist and Jesus begin their ministries in Galilee and along the Jordan River, unnoticed by Tiberius Caesar in Rome and his governors in Palestine.

Verse 1 can be read as the title for the whole book of Mark. **Christ** is a title, the Greek word for **Messiah**, meaning *anointed*.

READ MARK 1:1-8

1. Mark quotes Old Testament prophecy about a messenger who will come from God. Where will the messenger work?

   What is his task?

   What is his message?

2. In what ways does John the baptizer fulfill the Old Testament prophecy about the messenger?

Note: To the Jews John's dress signified he was a prophet like the Old Testament prophet Elijah. His food was that of the poor.

3. In what ways would John's ministry prepare the people for the Messiah?

How does repentance prepare us to receive a Savior?

READ MARK 1:9-15

4. Locate Galilee, Nazareth, Jerusalem, and the Jordan River on the map on page 109. Notice that Jesus walks over 60 miles to be baptized by John. What are the unique events at Jesus' baptism?

How are the Father, the Son, and the Holy Spirit represented here?

5. Imagine verses 12 and 13 as a large painting. What facts about the temptation does Mark emphasize by the setting, and who and what he includes?

6. After his temptation, Jesus begins to preach the good news of God in Galilee. What does this suggest about the outcome of his temptation?

7. What similarities and what differences do you see between Jesus' preaching (verse 15) and John's (verses 4, 7, 8)?

READ MARK 1:16–20

8. From what class of society does Jesus call his first disciples?

Why, do you think, does he not call religious leaders, scribes and priests?

9. How does Jesus change the focus of the work of Simon and Andrew?

What indications are there that James and John are perhaps younger and financially better off than Simon and Andrew?

10. What comments might the families or neighbors have made when these four followed Jesus?

What reactions would there be today?

READ MARK 1:21-28

11. In the synagogue at Capernaum, what impresses the people about Jesus' teaching (verses 22, 27)?

12. How does the unclean spirit address and identify Jesus?

What pronoun does the spirit use in referring to himself?

What does he fear?

13. How do Jesus' two commands make it clear that he regards the unclean spirit as a separate entity from the man it is possessing?

Note: Do not spend a lot of time at this point discussing evil spirits. Mark will mention them several times in his book and you will learn more as you study further.

READ MARK 1:29-34

14. How do the four disciples react to the crisis they find in the home of Simon and Andrew?

15. What events of this Sabbath day stimulate the crowd's activity at sundown?

Note: The Jewish Sabbath ends at sundown.

16. Once again Jesus refuses to let demons speak (verses 25, 34). What reasons do you think he has for this action?

READ MARK 1:35-39

17. On the Sabbath day Jesus taught in the synagogue, cast out the evil spirit, healed Simon's mother-in-law, and after sunset healed the sick and cast out many demons from the people the crowd brought. After such a day when, where and why does Jesus pray?

18. Why are Simon and the disciples looking for Jesus?

How is this a temptation for Jesus?

19. Why does Jesus set the priorities on his ministry of preaching and healing as he does?

Locate on your map the places where Jesus preaches in his early ministry.

READ MARK 1:40-45

20. Lest the reader conclude from verse 38 that Jesus does not care about people's physical needs, Mark records

Jesus' response to a leper. What question does the leper have?

What would it mean to the leper to have Jesus touch him rather than just speak to him?

21. How does the leper's disobedience of Jesus' strict order interfere with Jesus' plan?

*Note: The term **leprosy** included some other skin diseases as well as leprosy itself. Under Jewish law anyone who recovered from such a skin disease had to be examined by a priest and go through a ceremony of restoration (Leviticus 14). After receiving a certificate that he was clean, he could return to live in society.*

SUMMARY

1. How does Mark begin to prove his thesis that Jesus is the Christ, the Son of God?

2. What indications are there that Jesus is also truly human?

3. What impressions do you get of Jesus thus far?

CONCLUSION

Mark begins his record of the life of Jesus Christ with Jesus' public ministry rather than with his birth as Matthew and Luke do. Mark links Jesus to the Old Testament prophecies of Messiah by including the purpose and effect of John the baptizer's ministry. He begins to reveal who Jesus is by describing Jesus' baptism, temptation, and early preaching and healing ministry in Galilee.

DISCUSSION *2*

Popularity and Controversy

MARK 2:1—3:6

As news spreads of Jesus' authoritative preaching and his ability to heal diseases and cast out demons, many people flock to him. Religious leaders begin to scrutinize his words and actions with increasing hostility. Look carefully at how Jesus handles their questions.

READ MARK 2:1-12

1. Imagine you are making a video of this incident. Describe the setting and the characters.

As the scene opens, what is going on?

Note: Jesus had taught in the synagogue and healed many people during a previous visit in Capernaum (1:21-33).

2. What indicates Jesus' popularity at this time?

3. Why and how is Jesus' preaching interrupted?

How does he react to this interruption?

4. What do you think the paralytic's friends have in mind?

    How does that compare with what Jesus says in verse 5?

5. How do the scribes or teachers of the law react to this statement and why? Look up *blasphemy* in a collegiate dictionary.

Note: Under Jewish law, blasphemy was punishable by death.

6. In your own words what are the scribes thinking?

    What is the point of the question Jesus asks in reply (verse 9)?

7. What does Jesus expect to prove to the scribes by healing the paralytic?

8. How does the paralytic express his faith?

    How do the people react to his healing?

9. Jesus chooses a tax collector to join the four fishermen even though tax collectors were despised as thieves and collaborators with Rome. At Levi's dinner party:

> who complains

> to whom

> about what

10. In response to their complaint, what claim does Jesus make about himself?

What is he saying about the Pharisees?

Note: The Pharisees were a religious party respected for their piety who stressed strict observance of the law and the many, very detailed regulations that had been added to it.

READ MARK 2:18-22

11. Some people question Jesus as to why his disciples are not fasting. In answering them Jesus refers to himself and his disciples as a bridegroom and his guests. What do you learn about his ministry from this description?

Since one purpose of fasting can be to bring us closer to God, why do Jesus' disciples not need to fast for a while?

When will it be appropriate for his disciples to fast?

Note: In that time, wedding guests were exempt from all fasting during the week long festivities of a wedding celebration.

12. What is the *old* practice that people are discussing?

How do Jesus' illustrations (of what happens and why when the *new* is put into the *old*) answer their question about his disciples not fasting (verses 21, 22)?

What is the *new*?

READ MARK 2:23-28

13. What new complaint do the Pharisees make to Jesus about his disciples?

14. How does Jesus use an Old Testament story to answer their complaint?

What different purposes do Jesus and the Pharisees see for the Sabbath?

Note: **Son of man** *is the name Jesus uses in referring to himself. See Mark 2:10. At this time over a thousand man-made rules and regulations made the Sabbath a terrible burden instead of a physical and spiritual benefit.*

READ MARK 3:1-6

15. What change do you observe in those who oppose Jesus?

16. What do you learn about Jesus from this confrontation in the synagogue?

17. What are the results of this healing for the man and for Jesus?

Note: The Pharisees and Herodians normally would have nothing to do with each other.

SUMMARY

1. How and why does the degree of opposition to Jesus increase through each of these five sections?

Who opposes Jesus today, and why?

2. Consider what happens to the paralytic, to Levi, and to the man with the withered hand when they meet Jesus.

Why is their experience so different from that of the Pharisees?

CONCLUSION

Some people react negatively to what Jesus says and does. His claims of authority and his lack of conformity to the religious status quo disturb the religious leaders of his day. Early in Jesus' ministry they plot to destroy him.

DISCUSSION 3

Recognized and Misunderstood

MARK 3:7-35

J esus encounters growing popularity and increasing opposition. In this chapter, watch how the crowds, Jesus' disciples,
his family members, and the religious leaders react strongly
for him or against him. Look for what Jesus does to multiply
his ministry. Observe how he makes clear his identity and
the true source of his power.

READ MARK 3:7-12

1. What reasons might Jesus have for choosing the seaside
for his teaching?

2. How does Mark emphasize the size of the crowds that
are following Jesus?

On your map locate the areas from which the crowds
come.

How has Jesus' ministry grown since Mark 1:28?

3. Why is Jesus drawing such large groups?

4. What pattern in dealing with unclean spirits emerges (verses 11, 12)?

How does this compare with Jesus' dealing with an unclean spirit in Mark 1:23-26?

5. Why would Jesus not want publicity from the unclean spirits?

READ MARK 3:13-19

6. What does Jesus appoint the twelve apostles to do?

What is significant about the order of these three things?

7. To which three disciples does Jesus give additional names?

To whom do we usually give nicknames?

What does **Sons of Thunder** suggest about the personalities of James and John?

Watch for times later in the narrative when Peter, James and John appear as a select group.

8. What other special notations are made about the disciples?

Note: **Levi** *(2:14) and Matthew are the same person. A* **Zealot** *(3:18) was a member of a Jewish political party that opposed paying taxes to Rome.*

READ MARK 3:20–30

9. Why doesn't Jesus have time to eat?

What do his friends think about this?

10. What accusation do the scribes from Jerusalem make against Jesus?

What things has Jesus done which require supernatural power?

11. How does Jesus rule their accusation as illogical (verses 24-26)?

12. What further claim is Jesus making in verse 27?

Who is the strong man whose house is being plundered?

Note: Jesus has been driving out Satan's demons.

13. How have Jesus' accusers blasphemed against the Holy Spirit (verse 30)?

What is the source of Jesus' power (Mark 1:10, 11)?

14. What are the works of Jesus meant to reveal?

What do his accusers say they reveal?

Note: God only deals with women and men by the Holy Spirit. As long as people say the goodness of God is the evil of Satan, they will not come to God, repent and receive God's forgiveness. They cut themselves off from the only avenue to God.

READ MARK 3:31–35

15. Describe the scene in this paragraph.

16. What does Jesus teach is the basis of a relationship with him (verses 34, 35)?

In this chapter who meets this relationship requirement, and who does not?

Summary

1. What positive and negative effects of Jesus' activities in chapters 1 and 2 do you see in chapter 3?

2. If you were one of the twelve disciples, what warning and challenge would you remember from what happens in verses 20–35?

   How does this warning and this challenge apply to you?

Conclusion

Like a stone flung into a pool of water, the ministry of Jesus has increasing repercussions. The crowd squeezed into a home (Mark 2:2) becomes a great multitude (3:7 and following). The opponents who questioned in their hearts (2:6) now openly accuse Jesus of Satanic activity. In this hostile environment Jesus graciously offers a close personal relationship to himself based not on physical ties but on doing the will of God.

Teaching with Stories

MARK 4:1-34

Jewish teachers in Jesus' day often used parables. In this section of Mark's Gospel, Jesus tells stories of situations from everyday life to teach spiritual truths. A parable usually illustrates a single point in a way that is vivid and easily remembered. Jesus' parables move his listeners to think about what he says and then make their own decision to accept or oppose his teaching.

As you read this chapter, imagine sitting with the crowds on the lakeshore, listening to Jesus.

READ MARK 4:1-9

1. If you were an artist, how would you paint the scene in verse 1?

    What are the advantages of holding a teaching session in this manner?

2. What is Jesus emphasizing by his opening and closing statements (verses 3, 9)?

3. Describe briefly the four kinds of soil and what happens to the seed sown in each soil.

READ MARK 4:10-20

4. Who receives Jesus' interpretation of this parable? Why?

What does Jesus say that their concern about the meaning of the parable indicates (verse 11)?

Who has made the division between those inside and outside (verse 10)?

5. What happens to those outside who hear the parables?

Note: Verse 12 is a quotation from Isaiah 6:9, 10. William Barclay comments, "The Greek version (of Isaiah 6:9, 10) does not say that God intended that the people should be so dull that they would not understand; it says that they had made themselves so dull that they could not understand— which is a very different thing."

6. When Jesus explains the parable to those who ask the meaning, what does he say the seed is (verse 14)?

What experience do the four kinds of people share (verses 15, 16, 18, 20)?

In what ways do they differ from one another?

7. Jesus compares the types of soil on which the seed falls to the kinds of people who hear his message of the good news of the kingdom of God. Describe what happens to the seed in their lives when they face the pressure of the real-life situations he talks about.

Types of Soil	Life Situation	Growth of Seed
1)		
2)		
3)		
4)		

How do people today experience such pressure?

8. As you see what prevents a fruitful harvest in verses 17 and 19, give a present day example of each of these things.

Which are a possible danger in your life or in the life of people you know?

9. What variation occurs even among people who are good soil for God's word?

Since each of the four types of people in this parable **hear** the word, what makes the difference in their lives?

READ MARK 4:21-25

10. What similar thought is expressed both in verses 21 and 22?

If Jesus is referring to the purpose of parables, what does he say about them (verses 21, 22)?

Note: A common Jewish parable of Jesus' day told about Parable and Truth who came to town. The people ran and hid from unadorned Truth. But when Parable came, dressed in brightly colored clothes, they poured into the streets and celebrated. Truth complained to Parable, "I don't understand. Yesterday the people ran away from me. But when you told them the same thing today they celebrated." Parable explained, "People can't stand to look on naked Truth, but they will listen to it dressed in Parable."

11. How does Jesus emphasize the importance of paying attention, of listening to the word of God (verses 24, 25, and 9)?

What happens when you cease to give it your attention?

12. What things does the parable in verses 26–29 teach about the growth of the kingdom of God?

13. At what point is the growth hidden, at what point is it obvious?

How does this parable apply to the growth of the kingdom of God within an individual?

14. What is the main point of the parable in verses 30–32?

How does the parable apply to the growth of the kingdom of God in the world throughout all generations?

Compare the extent of Christ's ministry at this point in Mark's Gospel with its extent today.

15. What do verses 33, 34 show about Jesus' pattern of teaching?

*Note: The word **disciples** in Mark refers to a larger group than the twelve.*

SUMMARY

1. From this chapter what specific impressions do you have of Jesus' teaching?

2. Why, do you think, does Jesus emphasize the importance of the way you hear, the attention and response you give to the word of God?

3. In Mark 1:15 Jesus declared: **"The time has come... The kingdom of God is near. Repent and believe the good news!"** What do the parables in this chapter add to his teaching about the kingdom of God?

CONCLUSION

Listening to the teachings of Jesus is not enough. Obedience must follow hearing. The word of God must be allowed to take root, grow, and bear fruit in our lives.

5

Handling Crisis Situations

MARK 4:35—5:43

In this section of Mark's Gospel, you have the opportunity to observe Jesus as he encounters four situations of desperate need. Imagine yourself as one of those present—a disciple of Jesus, the person in need, or an interested onlooker. In each incident, look at the need that Jesus confronts, and how he handles it. Note briefly your discoveries in a separate column for each incident as you prepare for the group discussion.

READ MARK 4:35-41

1. At the end of a long day of teaching Jesus suggests crossing the lake. Sudden violent storms frequently arise on the sea of Galilee, furious enough to terrify even experienced fishermen. Why is Jesus sleeping through the storm?

2. What do the disciples imply by their question to Jesus?

3. How do Jesus' action and his two questions answer the disciple's question, **"Teacher, don't you care if we drown?"**

4. Why does this incident seem to make a deeper impression on the disciples than anything they have seen up to this point?

READ MARK 5:1-20

Note: This incident takes place on the eastern shore of the sea of Galilee. Being in Gentile territory accounts for some of the things Jesus does differently here.

5. What do you learn about the man's condition (verses 3-5)?

How would the people of the countryside feel about him?

6. According to Jesus' words in verse 8, who is speaking in verse 7?

What insight do these spirits invariably seem to have? See Mark 1:24, 34, and 3:11.

7. What new things do you learn about unclean spirits (verses 8-13)?

8. How do the people react to the changes Jesus brings to the demoniac and to their business? Why?

How does the demoniac react?

How do people today react to Jesus' power in these two ways?

9. How does the restored man respond to the commission Jesus gives him?

Why does this differ from Jesus' charge to the leper in Mark 1:40-45?

Remember that the demoniac lives in Gentile territory where Jesus is not having a continuing ministry.

READ MARK 5:21-24

10. Jesus returns from Gentile territory to the Jewish area. Who is Jairus and what is his need?

What faith does he have?

READ MARK 5:24-34

11. Describe the scene in this paragraph as you see it in your imagination.

12. What specific things do you know about this woman's condition?

What do you learn about the physicians of her day?

How do people today feel who have such experiences?

13. What does the woman know and believe about Jesus?

Why would she seek healing in this way rather than coming forward with her request as Jairus did?

Note: Under the laws of Judaism this woman's condition made her ceremonially unclean, and everyone who touched her would be considered unclean (Leviticus 15:25-27). Her illness shut her off from worship in the temple and ordinary social life.

14. In what two ways can people touch Jesus (verses 30, 31)?

What makes the difference?

15. What does the healed woman gain from her interview with Jesus?

READ MARK 5:35-43

16. Imagine yourself as Jairus. How do you feel:

as Jesus talks with the woman

when the messenger comes

when Jesus says, ***"Don't be afraid; just believe."***

17. Compare Jairus' reaction to Jesus with the reaction of the mourners.

18. Whom does Jesus allow to witness the healing?

How would Jesus' instructions help them to overcome their awe and regard the girl as a normal twelve year old and not a ghost?

SUMMARY

1. Over what forces does Jesus exhibit his power and authority in today's study?

What are the various reactions to his power?

2. What responses does Jesus desire from the people who come into contact with him?

CONCLUSION

In chapter 4 the disciples learned through parables. In this section they learn through experience in desperate situations. In the storm at sea they realize that the one they follow can control the forces of nature. They see Jesus' power to cast out evil spirits which were destroying a man's mind and personality. They see his power to heal a woman's chronic incurable disease and to restore life to a dead child. They see Jesus' power and concern affect every area of human need.

DISCUSSION 6

Jesus' Fame Spreads

MARK 6

Jesus' disciples have learned from listening to him, and from watching him transform impossible situations. Now Jesus gives them a taste of the privileges, the responsibilities, and the difficulties of being his disciples. As you see Jesus in very different situations in this chapter, what do you learn about his power, and his compassion toward those in spiritual and physical need?

READ MARK 6:1-6

1. Describe this incident as to:

   place

   people present

   reactions to Jesus

2. What is at the root of the townspeople's attitude?

   How does their unbelief affect Jesus' ministry in their town?

READ MARK 6:7-13

3. What authority and what special orders does Jesus give the twelve?

What reasons could there be to travel light, to stay in only one home in a village, to leave a place which rejects their message?

4. What is the common theme in the disciples' message, John's message (Mark 1:4) and Jesus' message (1:15)?

How will their ministry help to spread Jesus' message?

READ MARK 6:14-29

5. What do King Herod and others say about Jesus' identity?

6. How did Herod feel toward John the Baptist?

Why did Herod fail to accept John's message?

7. Why did Herod put John to death?

What things today keep people from doing what they know pleases God?

8. How do you think the disciples would feel when they return from their trips?

Why does Jesus suggest a day off?

9. What ruins their plans for a restful, quiet day?

How does Jesus react to this interruption in plans? Why?

10. When and why do the disciples want Jesus to get rid of the crowd?

How do they react to Jesus' challenge to them?

11. What indicates that the disciples have not considered their resources?

How does Jesus use what they have?

How do the disciples' jobs differ from what they originally had in mind for the day?

READ MARK 6:45-52

12. John 6:15 reveals the crowd's reaction to this miracle:

> *Jesus, knowing that they intended to come and make him king by force, withdrew again into the hills by himself.*

Why would Jesus not want his disciples to stay where the people intended this?

13. Why may Jesus need to pray at this time?

14. How is the disciples' day of frustration progressing by the fourth watch (3 a.m.)?

15. How does Jesus meet the needs of his weary, frightened disciples?

How would the events of this day help explain the hardness of their hearts?

16. We tend to think that if trouble comes to us it must mean we are not doing God's will. How does the disciples' distressing situation on the sea prove this idea incorrect?

READ MARK 6:53-56

17. How has the experience of the woman with the flow of blood affected Jesus' ministry?

Why does Jesus continue to be so popular with the crowds?

SUMMARY

1. What demands are made upon Jesus' disciples in this chapter?

What indicates that Jesus does not expect his followers always to receive a welcome and a hearing?

2. Jesus has compassion for the crowds which his disciples apparently do not share. How can you learn to have Jesus' compassion for people?

CONCLUSION

This chapter gives three examples of people who fail to receive spiritual truth. The *people in his home town*, influenced by a surface familiarity with Jesus which leads to unbelief, do not see him do any miracle. *Herod* misunderstands who Jesus is because he failed to act on John the Baptist's message. Jesus' *disciples*, though they experience his power in their own ministry, do not grasp the meaning of his power revealed in the feeding of the 5,000. They are completely astounded when Jesus comes walking to them on the water.

DISCUSSION 7

Tradition versus God's Commands

MARK 7

During the centuries after Jews returned home from exile in Babylon, Jewish religious teaching added many detailed comments to God's commands in the Old Testament. This chapter describes a major clash between Jesus and the Pharisees over what makes a person unclean before God. Look for what Jesus teaches about outward traditions and inner purity.

READ MARK 7:1-8

1. What reasons do the Pharisees find for criticizing Jesus' disciples?

   For them what is the standard of purity here?

Note: The disciples were eating with hands which were ceremonially defiled.

2. What accusations does Jesus make about the Pharisees?

*Note: The **Pharisees** were a religious party of the Jews that stressed strict observance of every detail of the traditional interpretations of the Law. **Scribes--teachers of the law** (NRSV, NIV) These* *professional students of the Law of Moses usually were members of the party of the Pharisees. They emphasized the importance of legal decisions made over many years that applied the Mosaic Law to daily life. By the time of Jesus, they considered this human commentary equal in importance to the written law given through Moses.*

READ MARK 7:9-13

3. How does Jesus illustrate the accusation he makes in verses 6-8?

Note: When someone pronounced **Corban** *(verse 11) on a piece of property or money, he dedicated it to God. This relieved that person from using it to help anyone else, but he could keep it in his own possession until his death.*

4. What contrast does Jesus draw between what Moses said and what they say?

5. What different things does Jesus say the Pharisees do with God's commands and with tradition (verses 8, 9, 13)?

How can you guard against substituting traditions or new philosophies for God's commands?

6. How do the Pharisees judge their own and others' righteousness or standing before God?

7. Jesus emphasizes the importance of this teaching by calling the crowd to **"Listen...and understand..."** According to Jesus, what makes a person unclean?

   What do the Pharisees think makes a person unclean (verses 1-5)?

8. What additional instruction does Jesus give the disciples about true defilement?

Note: The disciples receive this explanation because after the crowd leaves, they ask Jesus to help them understand. They also received the explanation of the parable because they asked (4:10).

9. Why, do you think, are **evil thoughts** the first on the list of what defiles a person?

   What is the meaning of each of the things that follow?

*Note: **Foolishness** (RSV), moral **folly** (NIV) is treating sin as a joke.*

10. Why is Jesus' analysis of the human condition as valid today as the day he said it?

11. If performing religious rituals doesn't make a person clean, what kind of cure do human beings need for inner defilement?

READ MARK 7:24–30

12. Locate Tyre and Sidon. What apparently is Jesus' purpose in going so far into Gentile territory? Compare Mark 6:31.

13. What do you learn about the woman and why she comes to Jesus?

Note: **Greek** *indicates her religion and* **Syrophoenician** *her nationality.*

What do you observe about the way in which she comes?

14. How would you explain Jesus' response to her request? Remember, tone of voice makes a big difference in the effect of what we say.

In verse 27 what does the word *first* suggest?

Note: **Children** *here refers to Israel which was to receive the first offer of the gospel. The word used for* **dogs** *suggests the household pets, an affectionate term.*

15. What suggests boldness and what suggests humility in the woman's response?

How does Jesus evaluate her answer?

What unusual element appears in this healing?

READ MARK 7:31–37

16. In this section and the previous one what difference is there in:

    location

    problem

    who initiates the interview

Why may the deaf man not have been involved in the faith which brought him to Jesus?

17. What are the specific stages in the healing of this man?

How would Jesus' actions begin to develop faith in the man?

How complete is the man's healing?

18. Why don't the people honor Jesus' request not to tell about this miracle since he granted their request to heal the man?

SUMMARY

1. According to Jesus' teaching in the first half of this chapter, what is every person's basic problem?

In your own words, state Jesus' definition of hypocrisy (verses 6-8).

2. In the two incidents of healing, what kind of response does Jesus seek and approve?

CONCLUSION

If a person's defilement is not an outward matter, his or her right standing with God cannot depend upon rituals or works. The cure for defilement, guilt before God, must treat not just the symptoms but the source of the problem, the human heart.

"Who Do You Say I Am?"

MARK 8:1—9:1

For many months, Jesus' disciples have watched him. He has taught crowds of people, healed different diseases, cast out evil spirits, controlled a raging storm, brought a dead child back to life, fed a large multitude. His disciples are beginning to discover who Jesus really is. Verse 29 marks the turning point of Mark's Gospel, and the title of *Christ* is used here for the second time in his account. Look for the new element and emphasis that now appear in Jesus' teaching.

READ MARK 8:1-10

1. At first reading this incident seems to be the same as the one in Mark 6:30-44, but what are the distinct differences?

2. In each incident Jesus acts out of compassion for the people. How can you express your concern for the spiritual and physical needs of others?

READ MARK 8:11-21

3. What sort of sign may the Pharisees have in mind (verses 11-13)?

How does Jesus respond to the Pharisees at this point?

Why?

4. Jesus warns his disciples against being like the Pharisees or Herod (verse 15). What attitude was typical of the Pharisees (Mark 7)?

What attitude or way of life was typical of Herod (Mark 6)?

How are these opposite ways of life equally dangerous?

5. How do the disciples misunderstand Jesus' warning (verse 16)?

What does Jesus try to make them recognize by his series of questions?

READ MARK 8:22-26

6. Who initiates this incident?

How does Jesus stimulate the man's faith by involving him in the healing process?

READ MARK 8:27-33

7. Locate the place Jesus now takes his disciples.

Note: Jesus keeps trying to get time alone with the disciples. The crowd ruined their day off (6:31) and a desperate mother found them near Tyre (7:24, 25).

8. What is the significant difference between the two questions Jesus asks his disciples?

If Jesus asked you both of these questions today, how would you answer each?

9. Review the focus on Jesus' identity:

Mark 1:11, 24

3:11

4:41

6:2, 3

6:14, 15.

10. How does Peter, speaking for the group, answer Jesus' second question?

After the disciples grasp and confess who Jesus is, what specific things does Jesus begin to teach them about the Messiah?

11. How and why does Peter react to this teaching?

How does Jesus' reaction indicate that the situation is ripe with temptation for him (verse 33)?

12. Why is Peter's response to Jesus' teaching about his death the human point of view rather than God's point of view?

READ MARK 8:34—9:1

13. What would the words *whoever* and *if anyone* indicate to the crowd and the disciples?

14. What do the three qualifications in verse 34 teach about the cost of discipleship?

Why does Jesus say to deny your *self*, rather than to deny yourself *things*?

*Note: Mark mentions the **cross** for the first time. At the time of Jesus, the **cross** meant the instrument of public execution by the Romans.*

15. What two possibilities does Jesus state are open to every person (verse 35)?

What is the only way to save your life?

16. What is the best that people living for themselves can do?

With what result?

Note: When Alexander the Great had conquered the empires of his day, he wept that there were no more worlds to conquer.

17. Why may some people be ashamed of Jesus and of his words (verse 38)?

18. How is Jesus' prophecy of his return in power and glory both a warning and an encouragement to those hearing his words?

SUMMARY

1. What things led the disciples to conclude that Jesus is the Christ, the Messiah?

2. What demands does Jesus make on anyone who wants to be his disciple?

Why is commitment only the first step of true discipleship?

CONCLUSION

After the disciples return from their preaching trip (chapter 6), Jesus tries to get away from the multitudes to question and instruct them privately. Now that the disciples finally grasp who he is, Jesus announces his death and resurrection and the cost of following him.

> **To prepare for next week's study, please look at the instructions for the review of Mark 1—8 in Discussion 9.**

Review of Mark 1—8

In preparation for the review discussion read Mark, chapters one through eight. Look for information about Jesus' identity. Discover what he says, what he does, and what others say about him.

Each person in the group should choose one review question for special study and lead the group in considering that question during the discussion. Two people may divide a question.

1. Describe John the Baptist's ministry and its effects.

    What is the core of his message?

    How does he identify Jesus?

    How does Mark's Gospel connect John with the Old Testament prophecy of Messiah?

2. What does Jesus teach in these chapters about:

who he is

his mission

his own destiny

3. What does Jesus teach about:

the kingdom of God

the Sabbath

the nature of defilement

being his disciple

4. What emotions does Jesus exhibit in dealing with individuals and groups?

What sorts of things does he do, and what do they indicate about his character? Give specific examples.

5. Describe Jesus' twelve disciples.

What do they see?

What do they learn?

Trace the progress of their faith in Jesus.

6. What positive and what negative reactions do individuals other than the disciples have toward Jesus?

How do you account for the varying attitudes of these people toward Jesus?

7. From the evidence presented up to this point in Mark's Gospel, what conclusion have you reached about Jesus' identity and the source of his power and authority?

DISCUSSION *10*

Belief and Unbelief

MARK 9:2-50

In the midst of daily work and ministry, Jesus continues to reveal more of himself to his often-surprised disciples. Read these incidents carefully. What do you learn about Jesus' identity, his future, and his power? Look for what he teaches about true greatness, and about the seriousness of sin.

READ MARK 9:2-13

1. If you were Peter, how would you describe this event known as the transfiguration?

2. How would the transfiguration confirm to the disciples the rightness of their confession in Mark 8:29?

Note: To the Jews, Moses was the giver of God's laws. Elijah represented the Old Testament prophets.

3. What time limit does Jesus set on the command he gives the three?

What two questions do they have?

They refer to the authority of the scribes in their second question. To what authority and to what subject does Jesus direct them in his answer?

4. To what authority should you direct those who question you on theological matters?

Note: See Matthew 17:10-13 for Jesus' comments on Elijah.

READ MARK 9:14-29

5. During Jesus' time on the mountain with Peter, James and John, what is happening to the other disciples?

6. How has the disciples' failure affected this father's faith (verses 17, 18, 22)?

7. Why, do you think, does Jesus discuss the boy's condition with the father?

   How does the father respond to Jesus' challenge to believe him?

8. What is Jesus able to do in spite of the father's mixture of faith and unbelief?

   What encouragement does this give when you must confess to a mixture of faith and unbelief?

9. According to Jesus' diagnosis, why were the disciples unable to handle this situation (verses 19, 29)?

What had they done instead of praying (verse 14)?

Rather than arguing about reasons for your in-effectiveness as Christians, what ought you to do (verses 28, 29)?

READ MARK 9:30-41

10. Why does Jesus wish to keep his travels secret at this point?

What is the reaction of the disciples to Jesus' teaching?

11. What different subjects concern Jesus (verse 31) and the disciples (verses 33, 34)?

Why are the disciples quiet when Jesus inquires about their arguing?

12. What does Jesus want his disciples to understand about true greatness (verses 35–37)?

How does this fit with your idea of greatness?

What does it mean to receive someone *in Jesus' name?*

13. What further insight does John's comment give you into the disciples' attitudes (verse 38)?

How may the incident with the deaf and dumb spirit have contributed to their attitude?

14. What is the point of Jesus' response to John?

What does Jesus teach about God's evaluation of deeds?

15. What does it mean to do something in Jesus' name today (verses 35–39, 41)?

READ MARK 9:42–50

16. In the four comparative statements, what is *better* than what (verses 42–47)?

17. In today's society how may a person cause a new believer or a child to sin?

18. How can one's hand or foot or eye cause him or her to sin?

If sin is this serious, what can you do to control your hands, feet and eyes?

19. What are the purposes and value of salt?

How would being like salt help the disciples be at peace with each other (verse 50) rather than arguing about who is the greatest (verse 34)?

SUMMARY

1. In this chapter, what do you learn about Jesus?

2. What do you learn about the disciples?

CONCLUSION

This chapter contrasts the mind of Jesus and the mind of the disciples, a contrast that emphasizes how alone Jesus was as he faced the cross. The disciples reflect our own experiences. As followers of Jesus we lack understanding. We put confidence in religious leaders rather than in Scripture. We are frustrated and defensive when we lack power spiritually, are fearful, and concerned for our own position.

11

Questions for the Teacher

MARK 10

As Jesus journeys toward Jerusalem and his predicted death, five different groups or individuals approach him with requests. What questions does he answer? Which requests does he grant?

READ MARK 10:1-12

1. When the Pharisees ask Jesus their test question, how does Jesus explain Moses' treatment of divorce?

Note: Moses' teaching was not to provide opportunity to divorce but to curb a bad situation and to provide some rule and order in this matter.

2. What does Jesus emphasize as God's plan for marriage?

   Why is fidelity the chief virtue of the marriage relationship?

3. In Jesus' further teaching to the disciples, how do you know that he does not set a different standard for men and women (verses 10-12)?

READ MARK 10:13-16

4. Why would the disciples rebuke those bringing children to Jesus?

How does Jesus use this incident to teach his disciples about the kingdom of God?

What does it mean to *receive...like a little child*?

READ MARK 10:17-31

5. What do you learn about this man in verses 17-22?

6. How may Jesus' claim (verse 18) be a challenge to the man's estimate of himself?

From the man's claim in verse 20 what does he think of himself?

7. For the commandments to which Jesus refers, read Exodus 20:3-17. The commandments not mentioned concern what relationship?

Those mentioned concern what relationship?

8. What does the man's failure to obey Jesus' two commands reveal about the one thing he lacks (verse 21)?

What is his god?

9. Jesus startles his disciples by declaring riches a hindrance to entering the kingdom of God. The Jews of that day believed that wealth was an indication of God's favor and blessing. Why is it hard, but not impossible, for those who have riches to enter the kingdom of God?

10. When Peter declares that he and the other disciples have done what the rich man would not do, what assurance does Jesus give him (verses 28-31)?

How are the promises in verses 29, 30 being fulfilled in the lives of people today?

READ MARK 10:32-34

11. What new details does Jesus give concerning the coming events which he did not give in Mark 8:31 and 9:31?

READ MARK 10:35-45

12. Compare what Jesus has on his mind (verses 32-34) with what concerns James and John (verses 35-41).

Why does Jesus answer their request as he does (verses 38–40)?

13. What shows that the attitude of the other disciples is no better than that of James and John? Compare 10:41 with 9:34.

14. What contrasting ideas of greatness does Jesus describe in verses 42–44?

15. Why is it essential for Jesus' disciples then and now to understand true greatness in the spiritual realm?

16. Verse 45 is considered the key verse of the Gospel of Mark. How does what you have studied this far in Mark illustrate the first half of verse 45?

What does this verse reveal for the first time in Mark's Gospel about the purpose of Jesus' death?

READ MARK 10:46–52

17. What is Bartimaeus' request (verses 47, 48)?

How does it compare with the request of James and John (verse 37)?

Why does Jesus ask Bartimaeus specifically what he wants?

18. Why is Bartimaeus healed?

Why is mercy the one request that is always answered by the Lord?

Note: **Mercy** *implies a kindness of forbearance, in excess of what may be demanded by fairness, forbearance and compassion.*

What do we indicate when we ask for mercy?

SUMMARY

1. How does Jesus answer those who put confidence in a *legalistic approach* to life (verses 2-9)?

2. What is Jesus' challenge to those who put their confidence in *material things* (verses 17-22)?

3. What is Jesus' teaching to those who put their confidence in *earthly position and power* (verses 35-45)?

Conclusion

The only people in this chapter who receive what they ask from Jesus are the children and Bartimaeus. The children desire his touch, Bartimaeus his mercy. We may have confidence in Jesus' answer if we bring these same requests to him.

Entering Jerusalem

MARK 11

Up to this point, Mark has given a rapid-fire account of Jesus' ministry. The story slows down as Jesus enters his final days. Recently he has revealed himself to his disciples as the Messiah (Christ). He has given them increasingly detailed predictions of what will happen in Jerusalem, headquarters of the Pharisees who are plotting to destroy him. This chapter tells about the events of Sunday, Monday and part of Tuesday in the week of Jesus' death.

READ MARK 11:1-11

1. What instructions does Jesus give to two of his disciples?

   What indicates that Jesus himself is initiating the triumphal entry?

Note: Riding on the colt was not a sign of humility but rather the sign of a royal person coming in peace rather than war.

2. How do the people react to Jesus' entry into Jerusalem?

   To what do the people look forward (verse 10)?

3. Instead of organizing an overthrow of Rome, which many in the crowd may expect the Messiah to do, what concerns Jesus after he enters Jerusalem?

   What pattern do Jesus and the twelve follow each evening (verses 11, 19)?

   Why may this be a safety move? See 14:1.

READ MARK 11:12-26

4. What happens on the way back into Jerusalem on the following morning?

Note: This is a difficult paragraph. Some scholars believe it is an enacted parable warning against show (profession) without reality. This may point directly to Israel and the temple worship in particular. Other scholars indicate that though it was not yet the season for full fruit there would be the early crop of green knobs or immature fruit which appear before the leaves if the tree is going to bear fruit later. Travelers sometimes ate this early fruit. Lack of any fruit at this point meant there would be no mature fruit in season. The leaves were a deception.

5. If you had been a witness in the temple, what would you have seen and heard?

   What impression do you get of Jesus here?

How would the profiteering in animals and in currency exchange in the temple affect those who come truly desiring to worship God?

6. What reaction is there to Jesus' expression of authority in cleansing the temple?

How do Jesus' actions here compare with the expectations of many that Messiah would exercise political authority?

7. How does the fig tree now conform outwardly to what it is inwardly (verse 20)?

8. What does Jesus teach his disciples about prayer upon this occasion?

9. Why is it essential that you focus your attention on the greatness of God rather than on the size of your mountains when you pray?

Peter has been impressed with the withering of the fig tree and Jesus says that even mountains are subject to God.

10. Why can you not pray properly with an unforgiving spirit?

11. What issue do the religious leaders raise with Jesus and why (verses 15–17)?

12. Why can't they answer Jesus' question to them about John?

What did John proclaim about Jesus (John 1:19–34)?

How would this have answered their question about the authority of Jesus?

13. What did John's baptism signify (Mark 1:4)?

Why is repentance essential as a condition for accepting the authority and lordship of Jesus?

SUMMARY

1. What claim is Jesus making about himself by his actions in Jerusalem?

2. How do you account for the various reactions to Jesus' claim?

CONCLUSION

Mark devotes the remainder of his Gospel to a detailed account of the last week of Jesus' earthly life. Much of the action centers in the temple, and everything Jesus says and does brings almost immediate repercussions. Jesus' triumphal entry and cleansing of the temple illustrate his claims and ultimate purpose.

DISCUSSION

13

Debating in the Temple Courts

MARK 12

Debates that began in the temple in Jerusalem (Mark 11:27-33) continue through this chapter. The religious leaders place ideological land mines for Jesus at every turn, but he walks right through their traps. Observe how he challenges them with his own questions, with parables, and with quotations from the Old Testament scriptures.

READ MARK 12:1-12

1. In this parable how do the tenants treat the servants and the son?

   How is the owner's son described?

2. What prophecy does Jesus make in the parable?

Note: In this parable the owner of the vineyard is God, the vineyard is Israel and the tenants are the rulers of Israel. The servants are the prophets and the son is Jesus himself.

3. To repeat the point of the parable Jesus quotes from the Old Testament using a different word picture. Who are the builders and who is the rejected stone (verses 10, 11)?

4. Why do the chief priests, scribes, and elders react as they do to this parable?

How has Jesus answered their original question (11:28)?

READ MARK 12:13-17

5. With what motive and in what manner do the Pharisees and the Herodians come to Jesus?

Why would they believe that their question is a perfect trap?

6. What does Jesus recognize about his questioners?

7. How does Jesus answer their question?

What things are Caesar's? What things are God's?

To what situations can you apply this principle today?

READ MARK 12:18-27

8. What does the Sadducees' disbelief in the resurrection reveal about their question?

9. On what two subjects does Jesus say the Sadducees are wrong (verses 24-27)? Why?

10. What Scripture and what reasoning does Jesus use to prove that there is a resurrection?

READ MARK 12:28-34

11. What stimulates the next question?

Why would a teacher of the law ask this question?

12. In what way is Jesus' answer a summation of the ten commandments? See Exodus 20:3-17 for the ten commandments. Jesus' answer is a quotation from two other portions of the Old Testament (Deuteronomy 6:4, 5; Leviticus 19:18).

13. What, do you think, does it mean to love the Lord your God in the way Jesus describes?

What does it mean to love your neighbor as yourself?

14. What does this teacher of the law reveal about himself in his response to Jesus (verse 32, 33)?

15. Why does the questioning stop here?

READ MARK 12:35-37

16. Jesus now questions the current teaching about David's relationship to the Christ. What wrong emphasis have the scribes apparently been giving in their teaching?

17. What relationship between David and the Christ does Jesus want to make clear?

Note: The people of Israel in Jesus' time held David in high esteem because during his reign they had been free and victorious. They expected that the Christ as Son of David would be a great political conqueror. Jesus does not deny that the Christ is the descendant of David, but he shows that the concept of the Christ which the scribes taught was much too low. Christs is not only David's son but David's **Lord.** **Lord** *is the regular translation of* **Jehovah** *in the Greek version of the Hebrew Scriptures.*

READ MARK 12:38-44

18. What six things characterize the religious leaders against whom Jesus gives a warning?

Which of these things must Christians be alert to avoid today?

19. Why is the leaders' condemnation greater?

20. How does the poor widow compare with the scribes and the many rich people?

How is the widow obeying the commandment in verse 30?

SUMMARY

1. What do you learn about Jesus' view of the Old Testament from his repeated use of it in this chapter?

2. If you had been one of the twelve disciples what especially would you remember from this day in the temple?

CONCLUSION

Jesus uses the temple, headquarters of his enemies, for his classroom. They exchange challenges, questions, and accusations. But even in this atmosphere one individual responds to Jesus with spiritual insight.

14

Things To Come

MARK 13

Do you sometimes feel as if the world is spinning out of control? Terrorism, wars, oppression by dictators, earthquakes, famine, persecution for one's faith, corruption in business and politics—these things are not new. The people in Jesus' day resented the domination of Rome. During his last week, Jesus prophesies about two major events, then future—the fall of Jerusalem, and his own second coming. He speaks in terms of Jewish history familiar to the Jews of his day. As you read this chapter, what warnings and what encouragement does Jesus give his disciples?

READ MARK 13:1-8

1. Why does one of the disciples initiate this conversation?

What does Jesus say about the temple?

Note: One of the wonders of the world of that day, the temple was built of stones as large as forty feet long, twelve feet high, and eighteen feet wide. It is little wonder that their size and splendor impressed the Galileans. The temple was destroyed in 70 A.D. at the fall of Jerusalem, less than fifty years after Jesus made this prediction.

2. What do these four disciples want to know about Jesus' prophecy? Why?

3. Instead of answering their question immediately, against what danger does Jesus warn them (verses 5, 6)?

4. What types of things will happen (verses 7, 8)?

   To the people affected, these things would surely seem to indicate the end of the world, but Jesus says, **"Do not be alarmed . . . the end is still to come... These are the beginning of birth pains."**

READ MARK 13:9–13

5. In addition to the general calamities what specific troubles does Jesus predict for his followers?

   What job will the Christians have?

   For whom is the message of the gospel intended? See Mark 1:1, 15 for previous references to the **gospel.**

6. What commands and promise does Jesus give to his persecuted followers?

Why would a person be tempted to be anxious about what he or she is going to say?

7. Why is the persecution described in verse 12 the hardest to bear?

What is the reason for the persecution and what response is called for (verses 9 and 13)?

8. From this paragraph what do you think the church should be doing in the world today?

READ MARK 13:14–23

*Note: The **desolating sacrilege** or the **abomination that causes desolation**, would remind Jesus' hearers of the prophecy in Daniel 9:27; 11:31; 12:11. They would also remember when Antiochus Epiphanes, the king of Syria, captured Jerusalem, set up an altar to Zeus in the temple, sacrificed swine on that altar, and turned the courts of the temple into public brothels (about 170 B.C.). In mentioning the **desolating sacrilege** Jesus warns that such a thing will happen again.*

9. What specific sign, warning and advice does Jesus give (verses 14–16 and Luke 21:20–22)?

10. Why do women and children suffer most during sudden calamity (verses 17–20)?

How and why does the Lord show his mercy (verse 20)?

Note: The Christians of Jerusalem did heed the words of Jesus and fled the city before its siege and subsequent fall in 70 A.D. They thereby escaped the siege and destruction in which 97,000 were captured and 1,100,000 died from hunger and the sword.

11. Against what danger other than physical danger does Jesus warn (verses 21–23 and 5, 6, 13)?

Why should you not be swayed by signs and wonders?

What forms do false prophets and false Christs take today?

12. How does Jesus say that his return (the coming of the Son of Man) will be clearly distinguishable from that of all false Christs and prophets (verses 21, 22 and 26)? Compare Matthew 24:23–27, noting especially verse 27.

READ MARK 13:24–27

13. What things does Jesus say will accompany the second great crisis event?

How does the change from **you** (verse 11) to **they** (RSV) or **men** (verse 26) indicate that the second event would be in a different age than the first?

14. How will Jesus Christ come again?

What will he do when he comes?

READ MARK 13:28-37

15. What further teaching does Jesus give about the timing of events?

How does verse 32 substantiate the thought that verse 30 does not refer to Jesus' second coming?

*Note: **All these things** in verse 30 is generally held to refer to the things foretold concerning the fall of Jerusalem which took place in 70 A.D. within the lifetime of those who heard Jesus speak.*

16. Considering the prophecies of the chapter, what comfort does Jesus' promise give (verse 31)?

17. What does Jesus' illustration emphasize (verses 33-37)?

SUMMARY

1. Describe the two major events foretold in this chapter.

2. In what practical ways can you keep alert, guarding against spiritual deception?

CONCLUSION

Those who disregarded Jesus' prophecy concerning the fall of
Jerusalem did so to their own peril. Some people today dis-
regard his words about his coming again in power. But Jesus
declares that history is moving toward its end. God directs
the course of history and its culmination.

DISCUSSION *15*

The Final Night

MARK 14:1-52

When Jesus comes to his last night, he chooses to be with his closest companions. It is the time of the Passover Feast in Jerusalem, when it is customary for the Passover lamb to be sacrificed. The table is set, the bread and cup are served. Put yourself in each situation described in this passage, seeing the people, hearing the conversation, feeling the emotions experienced by the disciples and Jesus.

READ MARK 14:1-11

1. What different attitudes toward Jesus do various people express in this section?

2. How does Jesus evaluate the woman's actions (verses 3-9)?

    What decision does Judas make, and why at this point?

READ MARK 14:12-26

3. What preparations has Jesus made in order to celebrate the Passover with his disciples (verses 12-16)?

Why might the mention of the exact address of the place be a danger at this point?

4. What does Jesus reveal to his disciples during supper?

What does their reaction reveal about them?

5. What is Jesus trying to teach his disciples in verses 22-25?

Note: A covenant is a binding and solemn agreement between two or more persons to do or not do something specified. In the Old Testament, God made a covenant with the Jews which promised them that he would be their God, and they would be his people.

READ MARK 14:27-31

6. What prompts Peter to make his boast in verse 29?

How is this an implied insult to the other disciples?

7. What does Jesus know about Peter that Peter does not yet know about himself?

8. Why does Peter make his boast and pledge even stronger?

What do the others do?

READ MARK 14:32-42

9. What insight do you get into the heart and mind of Jesus?

How and why do Jesus' disciples fail him?

How does he react?

10. What impresses you about Jesus' treatment of his disciples in his hour of supreme loneliness?

READ MARK 14:43-52

11. If you were a film director assigned to reproduce the events in this section, what scenery, props, costumes, characters, and actions would you use?

What major impressions do you want to make on those who will see the film?

12. What type of group is sent to arrest Jesus?

How does Jesus respond in the situation?

How are the words of Jesus in verse 27 fulfilled?

Note: Many believe that Mark is the young man in verses 51, 52. The Last Supper probably occurred in the upper room of Mark's mother's house. The linen cloth was probably Mark's bed-sheet. He may have been on his way to warn Jesus against the mob which he heard approaching through the night.

SUMMARY

1. What impressions do you get of Jesus:

    in the house in Bethany (verses 1–10)

    at the last supper (verses 12–25)

    at his arrest (verses 43-52)

2. What impressions do you get of Jesus' friends?

    What impression do you get of his enemies?

CONCLUSION

Tenderness and terror, intimate fellowship and stark loneliness, brave words and feeble deeds fill this memorable evening. We are gripped by the profound emotions of these last hours before Jesus is separated from his disciples. Jesus sees every action—by the woman, Judas, the other disciples, the crowd—from the perspective of his approaching death and the Old Testament scripture.

DISCUSSION *16*

The Two Trials

MARK 14:53—15:15

After Jesus' arrest at night, he is brought before the Sanhedrin that intends to prepare a criminal charge on which the Roman governor can try him. The High Priest presides over this seventy-one member Supreme Court composed of priests, Sadducees, Pharisees, scribes, and respected elders. Observe Jesus' demeanor at his arrest, and at his trials.

READ MARK 14:53-65

1. When the Sanhedrin gathers for this emergency night session, what problem does it have?

   How do the witnesses fail to solve their problem?

2. What indicates the frustration of the high priest in this situation?

   Which of the high priest's questions does Jesus not answer?

   Which does he answer?

3. How and why does the high priest react to Jesus' claim (verses 62-64)?

What actions do they take against Jesus?

How does Jesus himself determine the main issue of the trial?

Note: By proper procedure the Sanhedrin must not meet at night, or during a great feast such as the Passover. A decision must be reached at a meeting in the court's official hall within the temple precincts. Evidence from witnesses questioned separately must agree in every detail. The accused cannot be asked self-incriminating questions. Between a sentence of death and the execution, a night must pass to allow the court opportunity to change its mind. The Sanhedrin breaks all its own laws in the trial of Jesus.

READ MARK 14:66-72

4. How does verse 54 show that Peter is perhaps the bravest of the disciples?

5. How is each of the accusations made to Peter a greater threat to him than the one before?

What progress do you observe in the way Peter answers?

Why doesn't Peter leave after the first accusation?

6. What does verse 72 reveal about Peter?

How are you sometimes like Peter, a disciple of courage, cowardice and remorse?

What pressures do Christians face today like the pressures Peter faced?

READ MARK 15:1–15

7. Why do the Jewish leaders take Jesus to Pilate?

8. What questions does Pilate ask Jesus?

Which does Jesus answer and how?

How are the questions and answers similar to those at the trial before the Sanhedrin (14:60–62)?

9. What does Pilate mean when he asks Jesus if he is *the king of the Jews*?

10. How does Pilate hope to use the custom of releasing a prisoner at the Passover Feast to his own advantage?

Note: The name Barabbas means "a son of a father" in contrast to Jesus who is "the Son of the Father."

11. How does Pilate try to avoid responsibility in the trial?

What chain of command do you observe?

12. Why does Pilate fail to carry out justice under Roman law?

13. Read aloud Pilate's three questions in verses 9, 12, 14. What do they reveal about him?

What do the answers to these questions reveal about the chief priests and the crowd?

14. In what situations have you been tempted to please the crowd rather than stand alone against them?

SUMMARY

1. What impresses you about Jesus at his trials?

2. In each of the trials (14:53-65 and 15:1-15) how does Jesus make it clear that the issue is his claim to be the Christ?

CONCLUSION

At his trials, Jesus stands alone. His silence and composure condemn both the Jewish and Gentile rulers who fail to do what they know is right. The High Priest, breaking the Sanhedrin's own rules, asks Jesus directly if he is the Messiah. When Jesus answers clearly that he is, they judge him guilty of blasphemy, worthy of death, and bring him before the Roman governor. Although Pilate recognizes Jesus' innocence, he succumbs to the crowd's pressure and orders Jesus to be flogged and crucified. Of all the people involved in the trials, only Jesus remains in control of himself and does what is right.

DISCUSSION *17*

Crucifixion and Burial

MARK 15:16-47

Jesus has told his disciples that he will be betrayed and put to death. He has declared the purpose of his death, *a ransom for many* and *my blood of the covenant, which is poured out for many* (Mark 10:45; 14:24). The dark day Jesus predicted has now arrived.

READ MARK 15:16-32

1. How are the words of Jesus in Mark 10:33, 34 fulfilled in verses 16-20?

    What has Jesus already suffered before he is brought to the Praetorium (14:65 and 15:15)?

Note: Scourging in itself could be a death penalty, and few remained conscious through it.

2. If, as is probable, Simon of Cyrene is coming to Jerusalem to celebrate the Passover, what does he have on his mind when he is compelled to carry the cross?

Note: The annual spring Feast of the Passover celebrated the Hebrews' release from slavery in Egypt. The Angel of Death killed the first-born in the Egyptian homes but **passed over** the Hebrew homes (Exodus 12:23-27).

Although he does not know it at the time, how is Simon finding what his heart is searching for?

Note: Many scholars believe that Simon did become a Christian and that he is mentioned in Acts 13:1 and his family in Romans 16:13.

3. For the significance of the details of the crucifixion compare:

verse 24 with Psalm 22:18

verses 29-32 with Psalm 22:6-8

Why does Jesus refuse the drugged wine offered to ease the pain?

4. Why does Jesus not save himself as the crowd challenges him to do? Remember his words in Mark 10:45 and 14:24.

What indicates the chief priests clearly understand the claim of Jesus that they are rejecting?

READ MARK 15:33-41

5. What was unusual about Jesus' death (verses 33, 34, 38, 39)?

6. What is the significance of Jesus' cry?

Why must he suffer this ultimate separation?

7. How are Jesus' words misunderstood?

What does the people's speculation at a time like this reveal about them?

8. What does the way in which the curtain of the temple is torn indicate?

Note: This heavy curtain hung before the Holy of Holies. Through it the high priest entered once a year to make atonement for the sins of the people.

Why is the way now open to the presence of God?

9. This centurion witnessed everything that happened to Jesus from his flogging in verse 15 to verse 39. How do you account for his testimony?

10. Why are the women witnesses to the crucifixion but not the disciples?

11. Describe the scene between Pilate and Joseph as you see it in your imagination.

What do you learn about Joseph?

12. What specific things does Joseph do?

Why are the women observing his service?

Note: Joseph had to work quickly before the Sabbath began at sundown. All work was forbidden until the next sun-down.

13. Some scholars think that as a sympathizer with Jesus, Joseph may not have been summoned to the illegal night trial at the high priest's house. Never-the-less there is a strong possibility that he was present and later revealed the events of the night to the other disciples. If the latter idea is true, compare Joseph as one of those present in 14:53-65 with the Joseph you see in 15:42-46.

How do you account for the change in him from a secret follower to a committed one?

What would it involve for a person today to change as Joseph did?

Summary

Have each person in the group choose one of the characters in this chapter and describe the events of the day to a friend (e.g. as a soldier saw it, as Simon of Cyrene, as a Pharisee, or as a woman saw it).

Conclusion

So by virtue of the blood of Jesus, you and I, my brothers, may now have courage to enter the Holy of Holies by way of the One Who died and is yet alive, Who has made for us a holy means of entry by Himself passing through the Curtain, that is, His own human nature.

Further, since we have a great High Priest set over the household of God, let us draw near with true hearts and fullest confidence, knowing that our inmost souls have been purified by the sprinkling of His blood just as our bodies are cleansed by the washing of clean water (Hebrews 10:19–22 Phillips).

DISCUSSION *18*

"He has Risen!"

MARK 16:1-8; LUKE 24

Jesus' story does not end with his death and burial. Darkness and despair are banished by the miracle Jesus' disciples never expected. The power of death is broken by the resurrection of their crucified Lord. As you read the sections for this discussion, imagine yourself as one of the women going early Sunday morning to anoint Jesus' body, then as a member of the troubled pair on the road to Emmaus, then as one of the disciples in Jerusalem, and finally as one of the group in the vicinity of Bethany.

READ MARK 16:1-8
In all the great early manuscripts available to scholars the Gospel of Mark ends at 16:8. Studying Luke 24 along with Mark 16 gives a fuller account of the resurrection.

1. What do you think the women are saying and feeling as they approach the tomb?

What do they see and learn at the tomb?

2. Why are they not to be alarmed? Compare Jesus' words in Mark 14:28.

How do the women respond to the instructions given to them?

READ LUKE 24:1–35

3. What details does Luke add in verses 1–12 to Mark's account of the women's experience?

   Why do the apostles react to the women's story as they do (verses 11, 12)?

4. What are the two on their way to Emmaus thinking and talking about?

   Why are they so discouraged?

5. Why does Jesus call them *foolish* and *slow of heart to believe*?

6. Describe the Bible study Jesus has with these two people.

   Why would Jesus give this study of the Old Testament Scriptures before revealing himself to them?

7. Why do these bereaved disciples invite Jesus to stay with them?

8. When and how do they recognize Jesus?

Why do they immediately hike the seven miles back to Jerusalem?

9. What surprises do they and the disciples in Jerusalem have for each other?

READ LUKE 24:36-53

10. When and how does Jesus next appear to the disciples?

11. What does Jesus emphasize about himself by his words and actions (verses 36-43)?

12. What does Jesus want his disciples to understand about the Old Testament Scriptures?

Note: Jesus referred to the whole Old Testament by naming the three major divisions, the books of Moses, the Prophets and the Psalms.

What special advantage is given to them at this time?

Why is it important for Jesus' disciples, then and now, to understand the Scriptures?

13. What message are his followers to preach?

How and to whom? Compare with the messages of John the Baptist (Mark 1:4) and Jesus at the beginning of his ministry (Mark 1:15).

14. Why is repentance a prerequisite to forgiveness?

15. What commission and instructions and promise does Jesus give to his disciples?

16. What is the atmosphere of Jesus' departure (verses 50–53)?

Why are the disciples unafraid now to go to the headquarters of those who put Jesus to death?

SUMMARY

1. What difference did Jesus' bodily resurrection make to his disciples?

What practical difference does his resurrection make to you today?

2. Why, do you think, do the study and the understanding of the Scriptures play such an important part in this chapter?

CONCLUSION

Many call the resurrection God's confirmation of all that Jesus claimed and did. The fact that the Lord Jesus Christ rose from the dead becomes the major theme of the early church's message. In the book of Acts, the disciples who saw and touched the risen Lord Jesus risk their lives to announce the good news to anyone who will listen.

CONCLUSION

At the beginning of his account Mark declares that Jesus is the Messiah (Christ), the Son of God. Chapter by chapter, Mark relates Jesus' statements that he came to call sinners, to plant the seed of God's word, to serve men and women, to die and rise again. He details Jesus' actions in casting out evil spirits, calming wind and waves, walking on the sea, multiplying bread and fish, forgiving sins, healing the sick, raising the dead.

Mark devotes over one-third of his book to the details of Jesus' suffering and death because he wants his readers to appreciate the significance of these shattering events as they fulfill Jesus' statement that he came to give his life a ransom for many. *Jesus still calls for commitment and discipleship.* He presents *each person with a choice*—to follow Jesus and let him rule in your life, or to follow the pursuits of this world and in the end forfeit your soul.

Jesus calls people to follow him. You have read of the men and women of his day who did that. You have looked carefully at Jesus' life, death and resurrection. You have heard his teachings and his promises. *What is your decision about Jesus Christ?* Will you invite him into your life? Will you ask him to forgive your sins and become your Savior? Will you acknowledge him as your Lord?

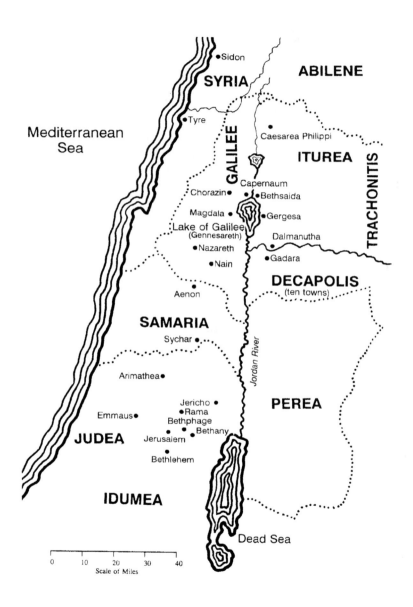

Mediterranean Sea

Sidon

SYRIA

ABILENE

Tyre

GALILEE

Caesarea Philippi

ITUREA

TRACHONITIS

Capernaum

Chorazin

Bethsaida

Magdala

Gergesa

Lake of Galilee
(Gennesareth)

Dalmanutha

Nazareth

Nain

Gadara

DECAPOLIS
(ten towns)

Aenon

SAMARIA

Sychar

Jordan River

Arimathea

Jericho

PEREA

Emmaus

Rama

Bethphage

Bethany

Jerusalem

JUDEA

Bethlehem

IDUMEA

Dead Sea

0   10   20   30   40
Scale of Miles

WHAT SHOULD OUR GROUP STUDY NEXT?

We recommend the Gospel of Mark, the fast paced narrative of Jesus' life, as the first book for people new to Bible study. Follow this with the Book of Acts to see what happens to the people introduced in Mark. Then in Genesis discover the beginnings of the world and find the answers to the big questions of where we came from and why we are here.

Our repertoire of guides allows great flexibility. For groups starting with *Lenten Studies*, *They Met Jesus* is a good sequel.

LEVEL 101: little or no previous Bible study experience
Mark *(recommended first unit of study)* or The Book of Mark *(Simplified English)*

Acts, Books 1 and 2
Genesis, Books 1 and 2
Psalms/Proverbs
Topical Studies
Conversations With Jesus
Lenten Studies
Foundations for Faith
Character Studies
They Met Jesus

> **Sequence for groups reaching people from non–Christian cultures**
> Foundations for Faith
> Genesis, Books 1 and 2
> Mark, Discovering Jesus *or*
> The Book of Mark
> *(Simplified English)*

LEVEL 201: some experience in Bible study (after 3–4 Level 101 books)
John, Books 1 and 2
Romans
I John/James
1 Corinthians
2 Corinthians
Philippians
Colossians
Topical Studies
Prayer

Treasures
Relationships
Servants of the Lord
Coping with Stress
Work – God's Gift
Celebrate
Character Studies
Four Men of God
Lifestyles of Faith, Books 1 and 2

LEVEL 301: More experienced in Bible study
Matthew, Books 1 and 2
Galatians & Philemon
1 and 2 Peter
Hebrews
1 and 2 Thessalonians, 2 & 3 John
Isaiah
Haggai, Zechariah, Malachi
Ephesians

Topical Studies
Courage to Cope
Set Free

**Biweekly or Monthly Groups may use topical studies or character studies.*

ABOUT NEIGHBORHOOD BIBLE STUDIES

Neighborhood Bible Studies, Inc. is a leader in the field of small group Bible studies. Since 1960, NBS has pioneered the development of Bible study groups that encourage each member to participate in the leadership of the discussion.

The Mission of Neighborhood Bible Studies is to mobilize and empower followers of Jesus Christ to introduce and multiply small group discussion Bible studies among their neighbors, co-workers, and friends so that participants can encounter God, grow in faith, and pattern their lives after Jesus.

The Vision of Neighborhood Bible Studies is to invite people everywhere to a relationship with Christ through the study of God's Word.

Publication in more than 20 languages indicates the versatility of NBS cross culturally. NBS **methods and materials** are used around the world to:

Equip individuals for facilitating discovery Bible studies

Serve as a resource to the church

Skilled NBS personnel provide consultation by telephone or e-mail. In some areas, they conduct workshops and seminars to train individuals, clergy, and laity in how to establish small group Bible studies in neighborhoods, churches, workplaces and specialized facilities. **Call 1–800–369–0307 to inquire about consultation or training.**

ABOUT THE FOUNDERS

Marilyn Kunz and Catherine Schell, authors of many of the NBS guides, founded Neighborhood Bible Studies and directed its work for thirty-one years. Currently other authors contribute to the series.

The cost of your study guide has been subsidized by faithful people who give generously to NBS. For more information, visit our web site: www.neighbohoodbiblestudy.org *1–800–369–0307.*

COMPLETE LISTING OF NBS STUDY GUIDES

Getting Started
How to Start a Neighborhood Bible Study *(handbook & video)*

Bible Book Studies
Genesis, Book 1 *Begin with God*
Genesis, Book 2 *Discover Your Roots*
Psalms & Proverbs *Perspective and Wisdom for Today*
Isaiah *God's Help Is on the Way*
Haggai, Zechariah, and Malachi *Prophets of Hope*
Matthew, Book 1 *God's Promise Kept*
Matthew, Book 2 *God's Purpose Fulfilled*
Mark *Discover Jesus*
Luke *Good News and Great Joy*
John, Book 1 *Explore Faith and Understand Life*
John, Book 2 *Believe and Live*
Acts, Book 1 *The Holy Spirit Transforms Lives*
Acts, Book 2 *Paul Sets the Pattern*
Romans *A Reasoned Faith…A Reasonable Faith*
1 Corinthians *Finding Answers to Life's Questions*
2 Corinthians *The Power of Weakness*
Galatians & Philemon *Fully Accepted by God*
Ephesians *Living in God's Family*
Philippians *A Message of Encouragement*
Colossians *Staying Focused on Truth*
1 & 2 Thessalonians, 2 & 3 John, Jude *The Coming of the Lord*
Hebrews *Unveiling Christ*
1 & 2 Peter *Letters to People in Trouble*
1 John & James *Faith that Knows and Shows*

Topical Studies
Celebrate *Reasons for Hurrahs*
Conversations with Jesus *Getting to Know Him*
Coping with Stress *Insights from Eight Bible Leaders*
Courage to Cope *Uncommon Resources*
Foundations for Faith *The Basics for Knowing God*
Lenten Studies *Life Defeats Death*
Prayer *Communicating with God*
Relationships *Connect to Others: God's Plan*
Servants of the Lord *Living by God's Agenda*
Set Free *Leaving Negative Emotions Behind*
Treasures *Discover God's Riches*
Work - God's Gift *Life-Changing Choices*

Character Studies
Four Men of God *Unlikely Leaders*
Lifestyles of Faith, Book One *Choosing to Trust God*
Lifestyles of Faith, Book Two *Choosing to Obey God*
They Met Jesus *Life-Changing Encounters*

Simplified English
The Book of Mark *The Story of Jesus*